www.randomhouse.com/kids

Library of Congress Cataloging-in-Publication Data
Perkins, Al.,   The nose book / by Al Perkins; illustrated by Joe Mathieu.
    p.   cm. — (A bright & early book ; BE8)   Reillustration of the 1970 Random
House: The nose book.
SUMMARY: Noses are interesting and serve many purposes, including the one holding
up glasses.
ISBN 0-375-81212-1 (trade) — ISBN 0-375-91212-6 (lib. bdg.)
[1. Nose—Fiction.   2. Stories in rhyme.]
I. Mathieu, Joseph, ill. II. Title. III. Bright & early book ; BE8.
PZ8.3.P42 No   2002   [E]—dc21   2001031928

Printed in the United States of America March 2002 10 9 8 7 6 5 4 3 2 1

The NOSE BOOK

By **Al Perkins**

Illustrated by **Joe Mathieu**

A Bright and Early Book
From BEGINNER BOOKS
A Division of Random House, Inc.

Everybody
grows
a nose.

I see a nose
on every face.

I see noses
every place!

A nose
between
each pair of eyes.

Noses!
Noses!
Every size.

They grow
on every
kind of head.

They come in blue . . .
. . . and pink
. . . and red.

Some are
very, very long.

Some are
very, very strong.

Everywhere a fellow goes,
he sees some
new, new kind of nose.

A nose is useful.
After all . . .
some play horns . . .

. . . and some play ball.

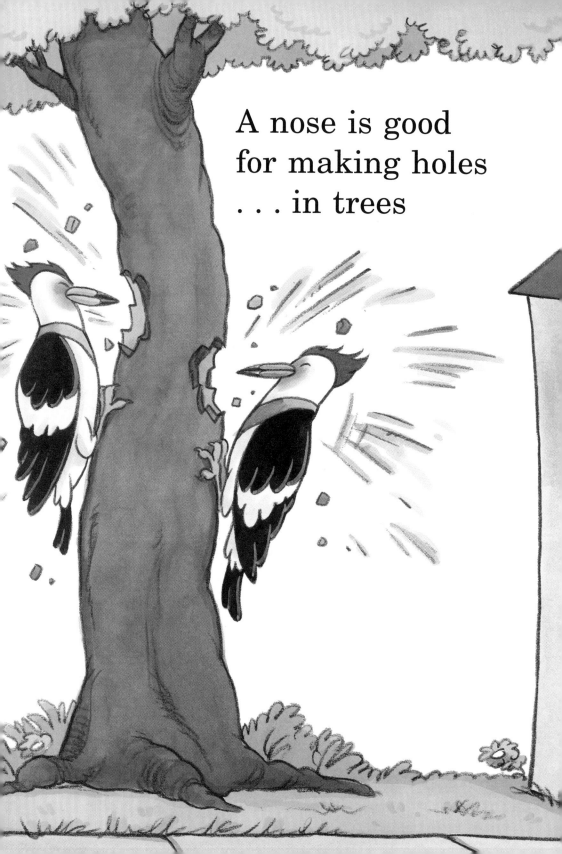

A nose is good
for making holes
. . . in trees

. . . and roofs

. . . and barber poles.

But sometimes
noses aren't much fun.
They sniffle.

They get burned by sun.

A nose gets punched . . .

. . . and bumped on doors

. . . and bumped on walls

. . . and bumped on floors!

Sometimes
your nose
will make you sad.
Sometimes
your nose
will make you mad.
BUT . . .

Just suppose
you had no nose!
Then you
could never
smell
a rose . . .

. . . or pie, or chicken à la king.

You'd never smell a single thing.

And one thing more.
Suppose . . . no nose . . .

Where would
all our glasses sit?
They'd all fall off!
Just THINK of it!

And that's why
everybody grows,
between his eyes,
some kind of nose!